My Next BMX Race Copyright

THIS BOOK IS DEDICATED TO ALL THOSE BRAVE LITTLE RACERS!

-AND A SPECIAL SHOUT OUT TO

WHEN I GOT HOME FROM THE
BMX TRACK

I GAVE MY BIKE A RINSE, AND WIPED IT DOWN

I LAID DOWN ON MY BED

AND THOUGHT, I CAN'T
WAIT TO **RACE** AGAIN!

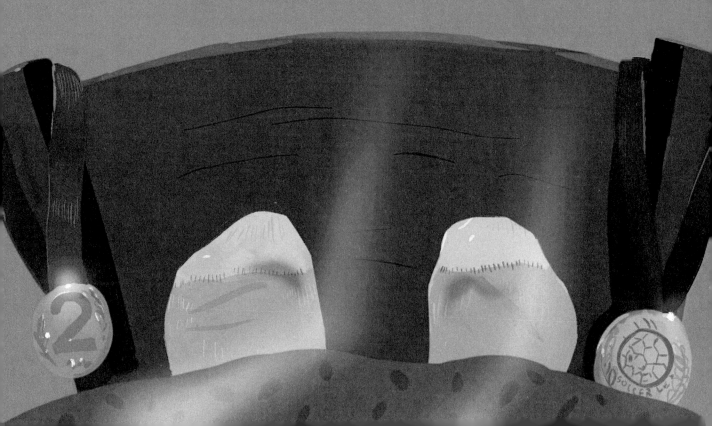

THE NEXT MORNING, I HELPED
MY MOMMY MAKE A HEALTHY BREAKFAST

I RODE AT THE SKATE PARK

I RODE AROUND MY FUN TOWN

I PUT ON MY GEAR

AND LOOKED OVER MY BIKE

HANDLEBARS

SEAT

FORKS

STRIDER

FRAME

TIRE

WHEEL

WE PRACTICED ON THE TRACK

AND GOT WARMED UP...

NEXT, WE LINED UP FOR OUR RACE!

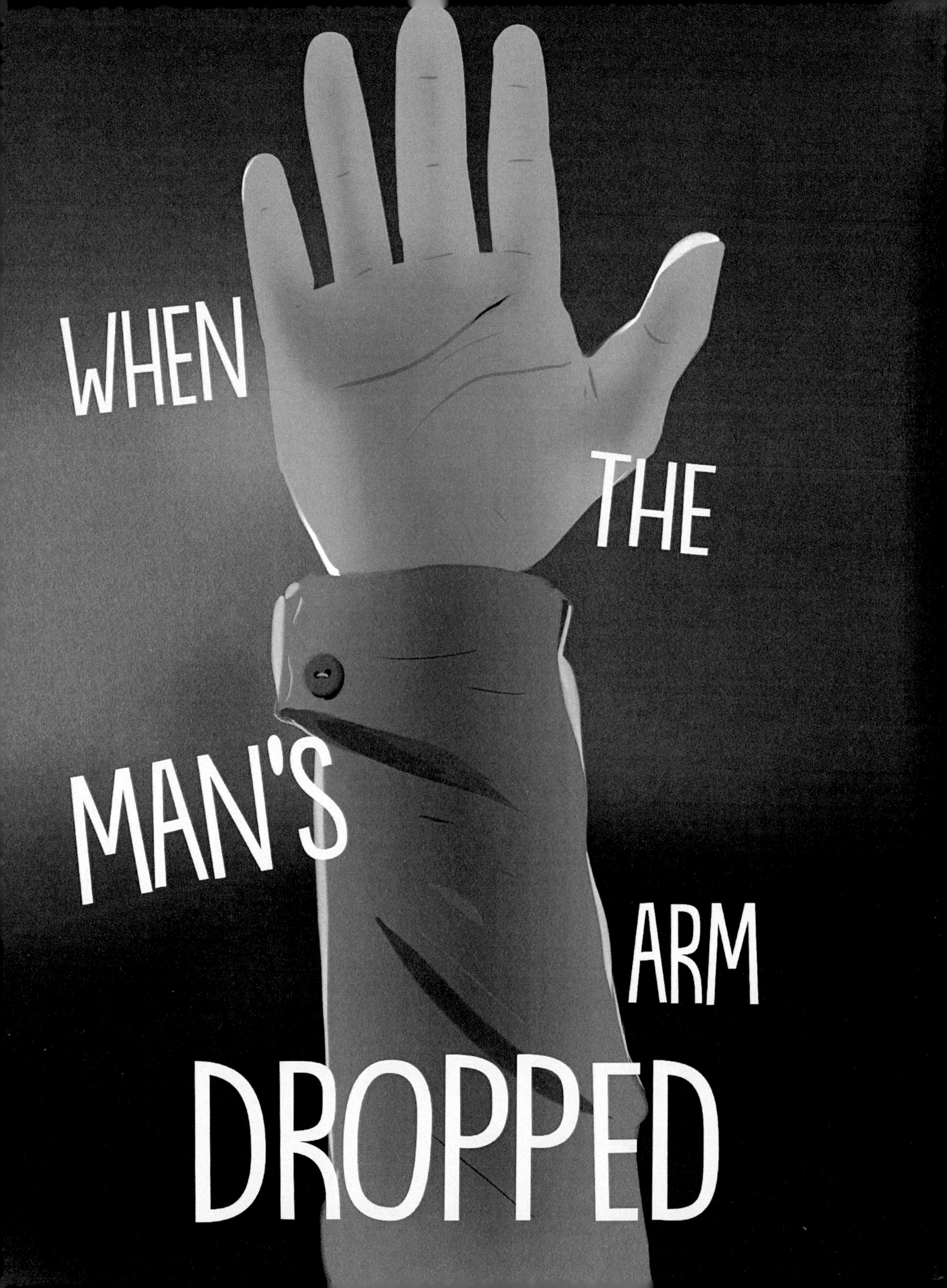
WHEN THE MAN'S ARM DROPPED

I WAS AS FAST AS LIGHTNING!

I COULD HEAR EVERYONE

CLAP AND CHEER,

AS I SPED TOWARD THE

FiNiSH LiNE

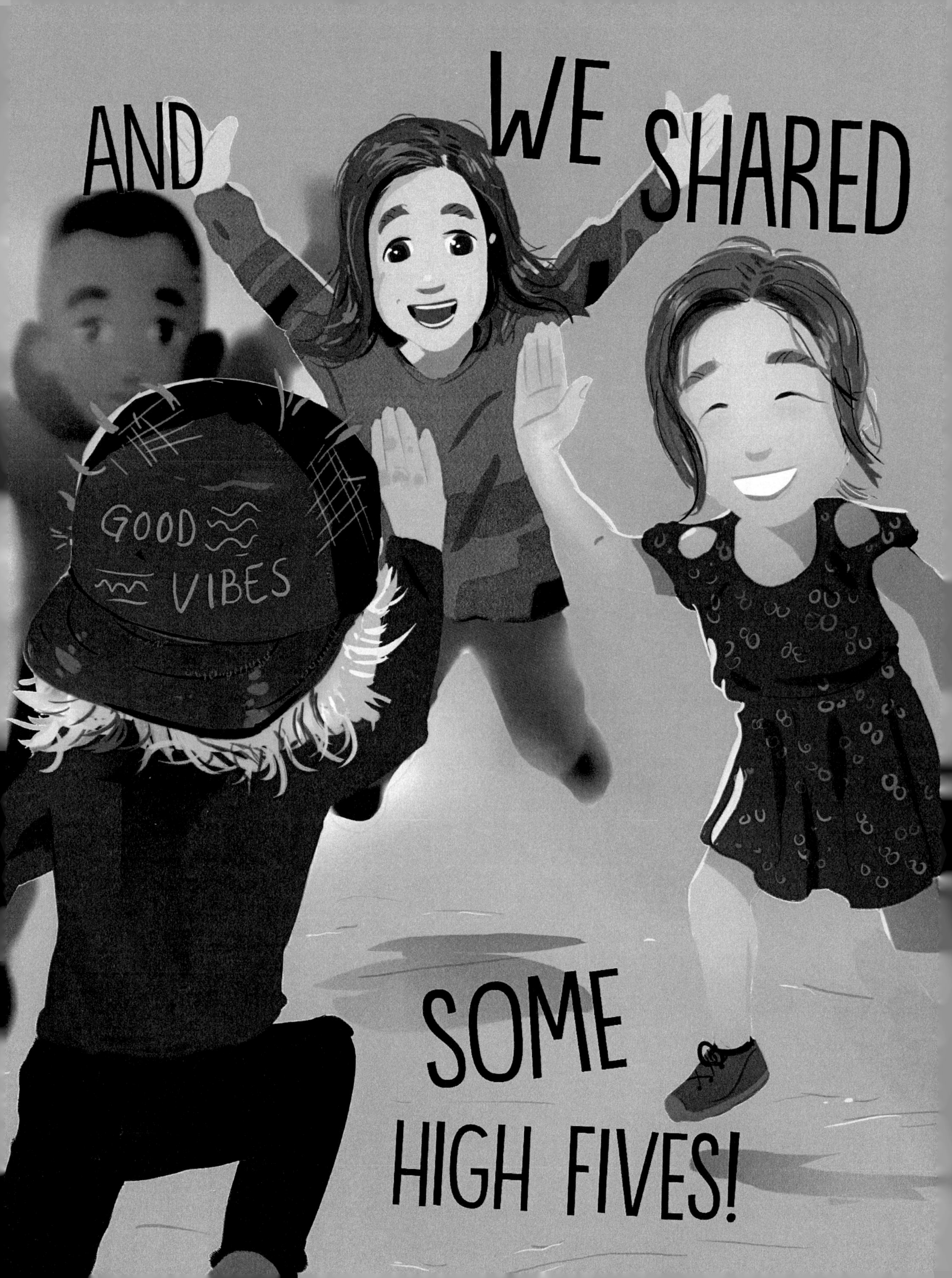
AND WE SHARED
GOOD VIBES
SOME HIGH FIVES!

I FELT **SO PROUD**

OF MY JOB **WELL DONE**

I SAT TO HAVE A TREAT WITH MY FRIENDS

AND WE WATCHED THE BIG KIDS
GET READY FOR THEIR NEXT RACE

I SMILED AND THOUGHT,
I CAN'T WAIT TO RIDE WITH THEM

BUT UNTIL I'M **BIGGER**,

I WILL KEEP **RiDiNG** AND **PLAYiNG OUTSiDE**

I WILL **EXERCiSE** AND BE **STRONG**

AFTER ALL MY PRACTICE ON MY BALANCE BIKE, MOMMY SAID SHE HAD A SURPRISE!

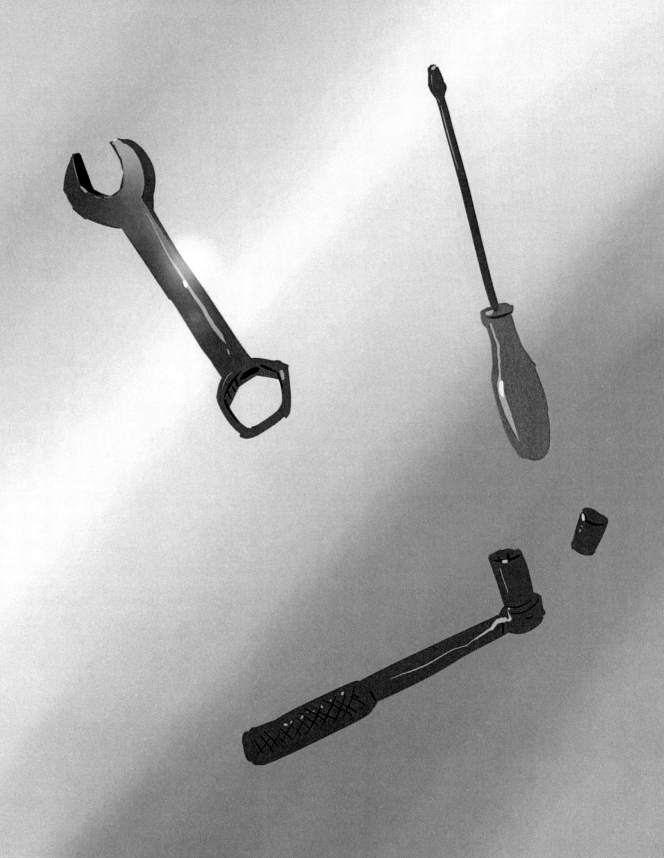

Try making these delicious and nutritious smoothies with your little racers!
Ingredients can be found at your local health food store.

THE LITTLE NINJA SMOOTHIE

BLEND:
1 BANANA (FROZEN OPTIONAL)
1/2 CUP OF FROZEN STRAWBERRIES
1/2 CUP OF FROZEN MANGOS
3 PITTED DATES
3 DROPS CHLOROPHYLL
TBSP MACA
TBSP CHIA SEEDS
TSP MORINGA POWDER
1 1/2 CUPS NON-DAIRY MILK OF CHOICE
(ADD MORE IF NEEDED TO REACH DESIRED CONSISTENCY)

Health Benefits: Immune system boost, clean energy, anti-allergy, protein source, healthy
digestion, combats colds, and full of vitamins and minerals

THE PEANUT BUTTER & JELLY SMOOTHIE

BLEND:
1 BANANA (FROZEN OPTIONAL)
1 CUP FROZEN STRAWBERRIES
1 TSP VANILLA EXTRACT
1 TSP MACA POWDER
1 TSP RAW HONEY
1 TBSP ALMOND BUTTER
1/4 CUP COCONUT MILK YOGURT
1 1/2 CUPS NON-DAIRY MILK OF CHOICE (ADD MORE LIQUID IF NEEDED TO REACH DESIRED CONSISTENCY)
TOPPINGS: SPRINKLE ON CACAO NIBS AND SLICED STRAWBERRIES

Health Benefits: Immune system boost, clean energy, aids in
healthy digestion, antioxidants, and is a great source of minerals and Vitamin C!

FEELiN GOOD PUDDiN!

BOTTOM LAYER:
1/4 CUP COCONUT YOGURT
1/2 CUP COCONUT MILK
TBSP CHIA SEEDS
2 DROPS OF CHLOROPHYLL
BLEND INGREDIENTS AND POUR INTO SMALL MASON JAR

MIDDLE LAYER:
1/4 CUP FROZEN BERRIES
1/2 CUP COCONUT MILK
TBSP COCONUT YOGURT
BLEND INGREDIENTS AND POUR THIS MIXTURE NEXT

TOP LAYER:
1/4 CUP FROZEN MANGOS
1/2 CUP COCONUT MILK
3 DROPS OF TUMERIC
BLEND INGREDIENTS AND POUR MIXTURE OVER THE MIDDLE LAYER

Healthy Benefits:
Antioxidant, anti-inflammatory, anti-allergy, protects against tooth decay, high in fiber and calcium, helps digestion, immunity-boost and clean energy

THE MERMAID SMOOTHIE

BOTTOM LAYER:
1/2 CUP FROZEN BLUEBERRIES
1/2 CUP COCONUT MILK
TBSP VANILLA COCONUT YOGURT
1 FROZEN BANANA
BLEND INGREDIENTS AND POUR FIRST INTO JAR

MIDDLE LAYER:
1/2 BANANA
1/2 CUP COCONUT MILK
3 DATES
TBSP MORINGA POWDER
TBSP VANILLA COCONUT YOGURT
TSP MACA POWDER
BLEND INGREDIENTS AND POUR NEXT

TOP LAYER:
DRAGON FRUIT SMOOTHIE PACK
TBSP CHIA SEEDS
TSP ACAI POWDER
1/2 CUP OF ORANGE JUICE
BLEND INGREDIENTS AND POUR LAST!

Health Benefits:
Cancer prevention, healthy metabolism, immunity-boost, vitamin rich, antibacterial, increase energy and endurance, mental clarity, stabilizes blood sugar, and is great for athletes!

AUTHOR

Since the release of her first children's book, Brittny and Sirian traveled to England, Scotland and Ireland! Together, they love to explore the Earth, meet kind people, and gain inspiration for new stories!

www.StarseedStory.com

@StarseedStory

ILLUSTRATOR

Edward likes to ride bicycles and draw when he's not eating burritos! To see more of his artwork visit www.ArtofEdwardDennis.com.

@EduardoDenniz

Made in the USA
San Bernardino, CA
19 August 2019